D1757860

ENGLISH
PRACTICE TEST PAPERS

Book 1

11+
ENGLISH

FOR GL ASSESSMENT

4 MULTIPLE CHOICE PRACTICE TEST PAPERS

NICK BARBER

Introduction

The 11+ tests

In most cases, the 11+ selection tests are set by GL Assessment (NFER), CEM (The University of Durham) or the individual school. You should be able to find out which tests your child will be taking on the website of the school they are applying to or from the local authority.

These single subject practice test papers are designed to reflect the style of GL Assessment tests, but provide useful practice and preparation for all 11+ tests and common entrance exams.

The score achieved on these test papers is no guarantee that your child will achieve a score of the same standard on the formal tests. Other factors, such as the standard of responses from all pupils who took the test, will determine their success in the formal examination.

Letts also publishes practice test papers, in partnership with The 11 Plus Tutoring Academy, to support preparation for the CEM tests.

Contents

This book contains:

- four practice papers – Tests A, B, C and D

- a multiple-choice answer sheet for each test

- a complete set of answers, including explanations.

Further multiple-choice answer sheets can be downloaded from our website so that you can reuse these papers: letts-revision.co.uk/11+

English

English tests are used by schools to assess the ability of each child and determine whether they have attained the required standard of English skills, including reading comprehension, vocabulary, grammar, spelling and punctuation.

Getting ready for the tests

Spend some time talking with your child before they take the tests, so that they understand the purpose of the practice papers and how doing them will help them to prepare for the actual exam.

Agree with your child a good time to take the practice papers. This should be when they are fresh and alert. You also need to find a good place to work, a place that is comfortable and free from distractions. Being able to see a clock is helpful as they learn how to pace themselves.

Explain how they may find some parts easy and others more challenging, but that they need to have a go at every question. If they 'get stuck' on a question, they should just mark it with an asterisk and carry on. At the end of the paper, they may have time to go back and try again.

Multiple-choice tests

For this style of test, the answers are recorded on a separate answer sheet and not in the book. This answer sheet will be marked by a computer in the actual exam, so it is important that it is used correctly. Answers should be indicated by drawing a clear pencil line through the appropriate box and there should be no other marks. If your child indicates one answer and then wants to change their response, the first mark must be fully rubbed out. Practising with an answer sheet now will reduce the chance of your child getting anxious or confused during the actual test.

How much time should be given?

Allowing 50 minutes for each of these practice papers will give your child experience of the most likely test format. If your child has not finished after 50 minutes, ask them to draw a line to indicate where they are on the paper at that time, and allow them to finish. This allows them to practise every question type, as well as allowing you to get a score showing how many were correctly answered in the time available. It will also help you and your child to think about ways to increase speed of working if this is an area that your child finds difficult. If your child completes the paper in less than 50 minutes, encourage them to go through and check their answers carefully.

Marking

The answers are included at the back of the book. Award one mark for each correct answer. Half marks are not allowed. No marks are deducted for wrong answers.

Using the results

Look for trends in your child's performance – are there certain kinds of questions that they have difficulty with? If so, then discuss ways that they might address their performance in those areas. Offer feedback in a constructive, helpful way. For example, it may be that your child needs to read more fiction books and look up words that they don't know, in order to improve their vocabulary.

And finally…

Let your child know that tests are just one part of school life and that doing their best is what matters. Plan a fun incentive for after the 11+ tests, such as a day out.

Contents

ACKNOWLEDGEMENTS

The author and publisher are grateful to the copyright holders for permission to use quoted materials and images.

Every effort has been made to trace copyright holders and obtain their permission for the use of copyright material. The author and publisher will gladly receive information enabling them to rectify any error or omission in subsequent editions. All facts are correct at time of going to press.

Published by Letts Educational
An imprint of HarperCollins*Publishers*
1 London Bridge Street
London SE1 9GF

ISBN 9781844198382

First published 2010
This edition 2015

10 9 8 7 6

Text, design and Illustration
© Letts Educational, an imprint of HarperCollins*Publishers* Ltd

All rights reserved. No part of this publication may be reproduced, stored in a retrieval system, or transmitted, in any form or by any means, electronic, mechanical, photocopying, recording or otherwise, without the prior permission of Letts Educational.

British Library Cataloguing in Publication Data.

A CIP record of this book is available from the British Library.

Commissioning Editor: Rebecca Skinner
Author: Nick Barber
Project Manager: Michael Appleton
Editorial: Catherine Dakin
Cover Design: Paul Oates
Printed in China

English

Multiple-Choice
Practice Test A

Read these instructions carefully:

1. You must not open or turn over this booklet until you are told to do so.

2. The booklet contains a passage for you to read and some questions for you to answer. You can refer to the passage to check your answers as many times as you want. You will then need to complete some spelling, punctuation and grammar exercises.

3. This is a multiple-choice test, so select your answer from the options on the answer sheet. Mark only **one** answer for each question.

4. Make sure you draw a line firmly through the rectangle next to your answer. If you make a mistake, rub it out as well as you can and mark your new answer.

5. Try to do as many questions as you can. If you find that you cannot do a question, do not waste time on it and simply go on to the next one. If you are stuck on a question, choose the answer that you think is best.

6. Do all rough working on a separate sheet of paper.

7. You have 50 minutes to complete the test.

Read the following passage carefully, then answer the questions.

The Story of Jean Lafitte

A Pirate's Tale

1 The story of Jean Lafitte goes back to the early nineteenth century. It was a time when America was fought over by men from many different countries for many different reasons. In the south of what we now call the United States, there was an area that was known as the 'Neutral Strip', a place between the areas claimed by countries like France and Spain, where lawless men would take refuge and try to make their fortune in whatever way they could. Jean Lafitte was one of those men.

2 Jean Lafitte lived in an area that we now know as Louisiana – an area filled with murky swamps, alligators, cypress trees and strange insects, birds and wildlife. It was an area that few men ventured into, as it was so difficult to navigate through and also very hot and uncomfortable. It meant that a man could create his own laws without too much fear of getting caught.

3 Jean Lafitte made a lot of his money by raiding ships in the Gulf of Mexico – he captured slave ships and took the slaves to one of several bases that he had established on remote islands. He was so successful that his bases did not have enough room for all the men and goods that he had captured – so Jean Lafitte decided that he would set up bases in the swamps of the 'Neutral Strip'. He would then sell his slaves and goods directly to the plantation owners in Louisiana.

4 Lafitte had many allies – other pirates and men in search of a profit joined his operation and set up their own bases. These bases, originally set up for the trade of stolen goods, actually had a positive impact in establishing crossing points on rivers and trading posts for the few locals who lived in the swamps. It was from this that Lafitte gained some popular sympathy, despite the dark trade that he was involved in.

5 It was around this time that the legend of Jean Lafitte started to grow – tales of where he kept his money and riches started to spread. Landmarks were given names – 'Money Hill', 'Contraband Bayou' – which created an air of mystery that there was buried or hidden treasure there in the swamps.

6 Even though he was a slave trader, Jean Lafitte knew how to keep the people he needed on his side. He was renowned for giving what were then regarded as quite expensive gifts, even though some of these gifts were sometimes stolen back again!

7 Lafitte also helped people to escape from persecution in their own countries – in particular, he helped French noblemen to escape the guillotine and establish a new life in Louisiana.

8 One legend has it that Lafitte's reputation was so great that he was asked to go on a secret mission to France to rescue Napoleon's fortune after the Battle of Waterloo. Napoleon was supposed to meet up with his

treasure in Bordeaux and then escape to Louisiana with Lafitte and his men – but Napoleon didn't turn up on time, so Lafitte sailed away with the treasure...

9 There were no grudges borne by Napoleon's men though – in the years following the battle, there were many stories of Napoleon's men finding a warm welcome in Lafitte territory in Louisiana, especially if they brought supplies of meat and drink with them.

10 Many stories and legends exist of men who had been involved in Lafitte's escapades, but they are very difficult to prove, because such men feared for their lives if they were to tell all that they knew. In particular, men such as Lafitte's slave cook, Catalon, obviously knew a great deal about the treasure that Lafitte had hidden around the swamps and bayous, but wouldn't tell. Catalon lived to the ripe old age of 94, but only shared a few tantalising stories about what he knew.

11 One story that he told was about some men from the city of New Orleans, who came to Contraband Bayou in search of treasure. They took out various strange instruments and maps and took measurements. After double-checking their measurements, they rode off into the swamps on their big, powerful horses. A day or so later, both men returned – riding the same horse. On the second horse was piled the treasure they had found – gold, jewels and other riches.

12 That wasn't the end of the story though – a couple of days after the men left, one of Catalon's friends had wandered into the swamps in order to fish and hunt, when he came across a disturbed patch of earth, around which flies were buzzing. Upon looking closer, he saw that there was a hole that had been dug out and deep in the hole was a skeleton, still dressed in the clothing of a sea-going man, with a shovel in his hand...

13 Perhaps it wasn't surprising that Catalon kept very quiet about what he'd seen and heard about the hiding of Jean Lafitte's treasure. Did he know where the treasure was? We can only guess – he certainly didn't leave any written down stories behind, only rumours and handed-down hints.

14 Some evidence of Lafitte's activities does remain. In the late 19th century, the remains of one of his old forts at a place called, spookily, 'Dead Man's Lake' could still be seen, saved from being washed away by flood prevention measures – but there were no signs of any gold.

15 Many stories and ghostly rumours still live on to this day, about the places where his treasure was rumoured to be. The stories usually have eerie associations – there is often a mysterious glow around the place where the gold is supposed to be hidden or often there are rumours of dangerous snakes who will attack the unprepared treasure-seeker, or even tales of cutlass-waving apparitions!

16 Today, Jean Lafitte is long gone, but certainly not forgotten. In New Orleans, buildings and streets are named after him and in Louisiana there is even a national park named in his honour, which has its headquarters in modern day Eunice. The dark deeds that he probably committed have been romanticised and have become legends, distorted by the exaggerating mists of time.

17 Today, treasure seekers still hold out hope that they may find some left-over gold; metal detectors, radar and all sorts of clever technology have been used to search for lost gold, but the swamp is still large, the alligators still guard their territory and so Lafitte's secrets will probably remain secret for a long time yet.

Now answer these questions, looking at the passage again if you need to. Choose the most suitable answer in each case. Mark it on your answer sheet.

1. The story is called *A Pirate's Tale*. What does that mean in this case?

   A It is a story told by a pirate.

   B It is a story about a pirate.

   C It is a story that has been made up.

   D It is a story about a pirate's pet.

   E It is a story that has been stolen.

2. Which one of these is true?

   A The 'Neutral Strip' was land that was owned by France.

   B The 'Neutral Strip' was land that was owned by Spain.

   C The 'Neutral Strip' was land that was owned by France and Spain.

   D The 'Neutral Strip' was land that was owned by neither France nor Spain.

   E The 'Neutral Strip' was completely owned by Jean Lafitte.

3. Why did few people live in the 'Neutral Strip'?

   A It was in the deep south of America.

   B Pirates lived there.

   C It was hard to find your way around and its climate was uncomfortable.

   D Alligators lived there.

   E You could get robbed.

4. How did Jean Lafitte make his money?

   A He raided ships and sold slaves.

   B He set up bases on remote islands.

   C He created crossing places in the swamps.

   D He founded towns for the settlers.

   E He worked for the plantation owners.

5. What does 'actually had a positive impact' suggest?

   A That everything that happened was good.

   B That everything that happened was bad.

   C That, despite being bad, Jean Lafitte's work had some good effects.

   D That, despite being good, Jean Lafitte's work had some bad effects.

   E That Jean Lafitte set up crossing points.

6. What detail suggests that Jean Lafitte became a figure of mystery?

   A 'Lafitte gained some popular sympathy'

   B 'Jean Lafitte knew how to keep the people he needed on his side'

   C 'giving what were then regarded as quite expensive gifts'

   D 'Landmarks were given names'

   E 'the legend of Jean Lafitte started to grow'

7. Even though he was a pirate, what did Jean Lafitte do that gained him popularity?

   A He hid his treasure so people could find it.

   B He gave away stolen treasure.

   C He protected people.

   D He gave places names that were clues to where his treasure was.

   E He created mysteries.

8. Why did Napoleon hire Jean Lafitte for a secret mission?

   A To pick up Napoleon, his riches and his men.

   B To pick up his men from Bordeaux.

   C To pick up Napoleon and his riches and help him to escape.

   D To pick up supplies of meat and drink.

   E To just pick up Napoleon's riches.

9. Why were Napoleon's men welcome in Louisiana?

   A They didn't hold grudges.

   B They helped with the piracy.

   C They didn't get many visitors in Louisiana.

   D They occasionally brought gifts that included supplies.

   E Jean Lafitte liked them.

10. Why are the stories of Jean Lafitte 'difficult to prove' according to paragraph ten?

    A   The people who knew the truth were scared of revealing what they knew.

    B   Not many people knew what he did.

    C   All the people who knew what he did are now dead.

    D   The people who knew what he did were murdered.

    E   The written information was lost.

11. Why did the men who came to Contraband Bayou bring 'strange instruments' with them?

    A   To tend their horses.

    B   To help them to find the hidden treasure.

    C   To weigh the treasure.

    D   To help them map the swamps.

    E   To draw maps with.

12. Based on the paragraph beginning 'That wasn't the end of the story, though…', what does the writer suggest that the men from New Orleans had done?

    A   They had dug up an ant-hill.

    B   They had dug up a pirate's grave.

    C   They had dug up the place where the treasure had been and a pirate was buried.

    D   They had made a mess of the swamp.

    E   They had disturbed some flies.

13. Why does the writer suggest that 'Perhaps it wasn't surprising that Catalon kept very quiet'?

    A   He couldn't talk.

    B   He didn't know what had happened.

    C   He didn't want to reveal where the treasure was.

    D   He was scared of what might happen to him.

    E   He kept the treasure.

14. Which of these ideas is **not** mentioned in the passage?

    A   There is a mysterious glow around places where treasure is found.

    B   Dangerous snakes will attack unprepared treasure seekers.

    C   Treasure seekers get eaten by alligators.

    D   Cutlass-waving apparitions are linked to the treasure.

    E   Men feared for their lives if they spoke about the treasure.

15. What impression does the writer give about his feelings towards the treasure?

    A   It is all lies.

    B   History and the difficult landscape have made it hard to know what to believe.

    C   Lots of people have buried treasure.

    D   He wants to go and hunt for the treasure himself.

    E   He doesn't want to go and hunt for the treasure himself.

16. In which of these would you be most likely to read a story like this?

    A   A leaflet.

    B   A dictionary.

    C   A magazine about history.

    D   An encyclopaedia.

    E   A comic.

17. Why is Jean Lafitte 'certainly not forgotten'?

    A   He has streets and a National Park named after him.

    B   His relatives still remember him.

    C   He is still alive.

    D   He wrote a book about himself.

    E   He lives in Eunice.

18. What does the writer **not** suggest in the last paragraph?

    A   There still might be some gold left.

    B   The swamp is large, so treasure is difficult to find.

    C   The swamps are dangerous, so people are scared to treasure-hunt.

    D   There is no treasure left.

    E   Any remaining treasure might not be found for a long time.

Now answer the following questions about the meanings of words as they are used in the passage.

19. The phrase 'take refuge' is used in the first paragraph. What does it mean here?

    A Look for treasure.

    B Hide from the law.

    C Build a house.

    D Take a journey.

    E Hide their treasure.

20. Which of these is the closest in meaning to 'persecution' in paragraph seven?

    A Being badly treated.

    B Being told what to do.

    C Paying taxes.

    D Living a dull life.

    E Being a traveller.

21. What does 'escapades' mean in paragraph ten?

    A stories

    B journeys

    C life

    D treasure burying

    E adventures

22. Which of these phrases suggests that Jean Lafitte's reputation has improved?

    A 'Some evidence of Lafitte's activities does remain…'

    B 'Lafitte's reputation was so great…'

    C 'The dark deeds he probably committed have been romanticised…'

    D '…the legend of Jean Lafitte started to grow…'

    E '…Jean Lafitte is long gone…'

Now answer the following questions about words and phrases from the passage.

23.   What type of words are these?

story   men   swamps   profit

A   Adjectives.

B   Verbs.

C   Adverbs.

D   Nouns.

E   Prepositions.

24.   'Catalon lived to the ripe old age of 94...'

Which of these words is a verb?

A   Catalon

B   lived

C   age

D   old

E   to

25.   'Did he know where the treasure was?' is a:

A   Proverb.

B   Joke.

C   Rhetorical question.

D   Summary.

E   Title.

In the following passage there are some spelling mistakes. On each numbered line you will see that there is either one mistake or no mistake at all. Find the group of words with the mistake in it and mark its letter on your answer sheet. If there is no mistake, mark the letter N.

The Journey

26. Once upon a time, there lived a man who liked to travel a grate deal,

    | A | B | C | D |

27. to countries far and wide, near and far. Their were many places

    | A | B | C | D |

28. that he hadn't visited but he wasn't worried about that. One magical

    | A | B | C | D |

29. land that he wished to visit was miles away over distance seas and mountains.

    | A | B | C | D |

30. He jumped upon his trusty hoarse and rode swiftly towards a large lake.

    | A | B | C | D |

31. The water shon in front of him as he rode onwards. The sun blazed

    | A | B | C | D |

32. fiercely on his uncovered head and he started to sweat profusely with the heat,

    | A | B | C | D |

33. but he knew that this journey was going to be worth all the effort and pane.

    | A | B | C | D |

In the following passage there are some mistakes to do with punctuation and capital letters. In each numbered line, you will find either one mistake or no mistake at all. Find the group of words with the mistake in it and mark its letter on your answer sheet. If there is no mistake, mark the letter N.

Fred's Holiday

34. Fred wanted to buy a new game. he didn't have enough money saved and
         A   B   C   D

35. so he went to his mum and asked her if she could spare any. She said I'm
         A   B   C   D

36. not made of money you know." Fred reluctantly turned and made his way up
         A   B   C   D

37. to his bedroom Once inside, he shut the door and got out his homework.
         A   B   C   D

38. He didn't really want to do work on the first day of the holidays, but he
         A   B   C   D

39. thought it would be better to get it over and done with. So that he wouldn't
         A   B   C   D

40. Be spending the rest of the holidays thinking about it. Suddenly, something
         A   B   C   D

41. fell out of the back of his exercise book. What was it
         A   B   C   D

In the following questions, you need to pick the most appropriate word or group of words so that the passage makes sense. Choose one of the five answers on each line and mark its letter on your answer sheet.

Painting for Money

42. Ellie sighed and started to clear the table. She

hadn't managed	hasn't managed	wasn't managed	couldn't managed	hadn't manage
A	B	C	D	E

43. to finish all of her paintings, but she

know	now	knew	knows	knewed
A	B	C	D	E

she could

carry on

44. tomorrow, when she

has	had	hadn't	hasn't	wouldn't
A	B	C	D	E

more time. Her last

painting had

45.

be showed	been showed	bin shown	been shown	been show
A	B	C	D	E

at a top gallery and

had been sold for a great

46. deal of money. She had bills to pay,

although	however	but	since	then
A	B	C	D	E

,

and needed to sell another

47. one in

order	ordered	ordained	audited	awe
A	B	C	D	E

to pay for the holiday that she felt

48. she needed. She placed her brushes

out of	from	in	to	towards
A	B	C	D	E

49. the sink, turned on the tap and let the water

flow	flew	flown	flews	flee
A	B	C	D	E

.

English
Multiple-Choice
Practice Test B

Read these instructions carefully:

1. You must not open or turn over this booklet until you are told to do so.

2. The booklet contains a passage for you to read and some questions for you to answer. You can refer to the passage to check your answers as many times as you want. You will then need to complete some spelling, punctuation and grammar exercises.

3. This is a multiple-choice test, so select your answers from the options on the answer sheet. Mark only **one** answer for each question.

4. Make sure you draw a line firmly through the rectangle next to your answer. If you make a mistake, rub it out as well as you can and mark your new answer.

5. Try to do as many questions as you can. If you find that you cannot do a question, do not waste time on it and simply go on to the next one. If you are stuck on a question, choose the answer that you think is best.

6. Do all rough working on a separate sheet of paper.

7. You have 50 minutes to complete the test.

Read the following passage carefully, then answer the questions.

Michelle's Holiday

1 Michelle was awake. That wasn't unusual – but what was unusual was that it was still dark. She usually woke, bleary-eyed at a decent hour, long after the sun had risen and the day had started in earnest. She rubbed her eyes and peered at the clock next to her bed. "5.07 a.m. …" she groaned.

2 Fortunately, she remembered why she was looking at the alarm clock at this hitherto unknown time – she was off on holiday. She'd been on several holidays before in her life, but this was the first time that she'd been abroad – the first time she'd flown on a plane too. This was going to be a good day.

3 "Are you up?" a voice called from below and Michelle sat up and stepped out onto the cold bedroom floor. She inched her way towards the bedroom door, pulling on her fleecy dressing gown to try and recover some of the warmth that she had left behind in her bed. "I'm coming!" said Michelle.
Michelle's mother acknowledged her from the kitchen and sounds of clattering cutlery and cupboard doors could be heard echoing up the stairs.

4 The cold water of the shower quickly caused Michelle to come to her full senses. After swiftly towelling down, she dashed back into her room, where she'd sensibly left her travelling clothes out, ready for a quick getaway. Fully co-ordinated and ready to face the journey ahead, she gave herself one last look in the mirror and bounced cheerily downstairs to her waiting mother. "Ready!"

5 Her cheerfulness caught her mother by surprise; she was still entangled in wrapping sandwiches and cutting bread into delicate shapes that would fit into small plastic snack boxes.

"Good. Can you go and help your dad carry the cases to the car? I think he needs some help."

6 Mr Wardle was the sort of person who needed help putting suitcases in cars. In fact, he often needed help remembering where the car was. Michelle was used to her dad's absent-minded quirkiness. It was actually the thing that she liked most about him. He wasn't like anyone else's dad. He was… different.

7 As she left the front door and turned towards the garage, Michelle could see a small greying figure wrestling with the difficult problem of trying to fit four suitcases into a space designed for three and a bit.
"Want some help Dad?" Michelle asked.

8 Michelle knew that he would accept. He wasn't a proud man and gladly accepted any help that was offered. His face appeared, squinting, from between pink and leopard-skin print effect suitcases. (Mrs Wardle had a theory that they would be easier to spot on the airport luggage carousel. Michelle wasn't convinced that this advantage outweighed the embarrassment of being seen in public with them.)
"Could you just hold this end of the pink one? Thank you. It'll go in, if I can just twist it over the parcel shelf…"

9 "Why don't you take it out? The parcel shelf? Then it would go in easily."
Michelle thought it best to offer her suggestion in a kindly way. After all, her dad must have got up before 5 a.m. in order to start this strange three-dimensional puzzle. She thought he needed to be treated tenderly.
"Oh yes… I never thought of that. What a good idea."

10 Within seconds, all four suitcases were in the back of the car and the boot was shut and locked. Much to Michelle's relief, the leopard-print case was firmly at the bottom of the pile of luggage and invisible to any neighbours who might be peering out of their curtains and wondering about the taste of the Wardle family.

11 Almost immediately, Mrs Wardle appeared briskly from behind Michelle, carrying carrier bags of provisions for the journey to the airport and simultaneously locking the front door with her few free fingers.
"Are we ready then?" she called cheerily.
"Yes, dear. Michelle sorted the suitcases for me," replied Dad.

12 That was another thing that Michelle liked about her dad – he was always so gracious with his compliments. Smiling, Mr Wardle took the lumpy carrier bags from his wife's grasp and opened the passenger door. His clearly excited wife slid in and started to quiz him about whether he'd cancelled the newspapers and locked the shed. Her questions were answered with a recurring string of "Yes" replies from her husband, who clearly was paying no attention at all.

13 Michelle settled into the back of the car as they reversed out of the drive and onto the cul-de-sac, narrowly missing a startled paperboy who hadn't expected activity from the Wardle household at this strange hour. The car swung around and gently started to warm up as they left behind their cosy estate and drove through the built-up, and slowly waking, roads leading them away from home towards the fortnight's adventure that lay ahead of them.

14 Michelle had been looking forward to this holiday for months – she'd loved studying the Romans at school and now she was going to visit the Colosseum, the Forum and all the other places that she'd only read about and seen faded old pictures of, in tatty school textbooks. Snugly tucked on the back seat between her mother's carrier bags of provisions and some sensible outdoor clothing, she took out a well-thumbed, plastic-covered guide book with its library ticket still sticking out.
"Is that a book on Rome?" Her mother was always one to note the obvious.
"Yes," Michelle answered simply, not wanting to prolong the conversation. She wanted to read.
"Does it tell you where you can get a nice cup of tea? I hear they only drink coffee. It'll keep me awake all night if I can't get a cup of tea."

15 Michelle didn't answer. She knew her mother tended to think out loud and wasn't upset if she didn't get a reply. Outside the car, the shops and streets swept past, giving way to the dawn-tinged greenery of the countryside. Michelle let her mind wander even further afield, to warm lands filled with centurions, togas and very, very straight roads. Soon she would be there and she wanted to be ready, to take it all in and soak up all that history and all that culture…
BANG!

16 There was a sound of escaping steam, a thunderous rattle from under the bonnet and finally, silence. The car came to a shuddering halt and Mr Wardle guided the shaking car over to the side of the road.

17 Michelle looked up from her book, firstly at her dumbstruck mother and then across at her anxious father. The flight was in less than three hours. They had to be there in under two, to check in. This was not good.

18 All three looked at each other. There was a silent understanding of what to do next – they were a family, after all. Michelle sat up in the back seat and rummaged in her jeans pocket. They were going to get there – and on time. If Julius Caesar could cross the Rubicon, the Wardles could surely arrange an emergency taxi…

Now answer these questions, looking at the passage again if you need to. Choose the most suitable answer in each case. Mark it on your answer sheet.

1. What was unusual about the time that Michelle woke up?

    A It was very late.

    B It was still dark.

    C It was a school day.

    D It was a Saturday.

    E The alarm clock hadn't gone off.

2. Why did Michelle rub her eyes?

    A So that she could read the newspaper.

    B Because they itched.

    C Because she wanted to.

    D So that she could see the bed-side clock more clearly.

    E Because she had an infection.

3. Why was Michelle excited about this particular day?

    A It was Saturday.

    B It was a school day.

    C It was her birthday.

    D She was going on holiday for the first time.

    E She was going on a foreign holiday on a plane for the first time.

4. Who is downstairs and inside the house?

    A Her brother.

    B Her father.

    C Her mother.

    D Her Gran.

    E Her sister.

5. In paragraph four, what information suggests that Michelle is a well-organised person?

    A   She had already made her own dinner.

    B   She had left her travelling clothes out the night before.

    C   She had a shower.

    D   She used cold water in the shower.

    E   She swiftly towelled down.

6. What had Mr Wardle been doing just before Michelle came downstairs?

    A   Making breakfast.

    B   Helping Mrs Wardle.

    C   Having a shave.

    D   Getting the car ready.

    E   Waking Michelle up.

7. Which of these statements seems most likely?

    A   Michelle is not as well-organised as her father.

    B   Michelle is not as well-organised as her mother.

    C   Michelle is not well-organised.

    D   Michelle is better organised than her father.

    E   Michelle doesn't like her father.

8. How does Michelle solve the problem of packing the car?

    A   She takes over.

    B   She gets her mother to do it.

    C   She tells her father to get rid of one of the cases.

    D   She tells her father to not be absent-minded.

    E   She tells her father what to do.

9. Which of these best describes Michelle's feelings towards her father?

    A   Angry, because he was so useless.

    B   Caring, because he'd been up early.

    C   Annoyed, because he couldn't solve the problem of the luggage.

    D   Helpful, because he wasn't very clever.

    E   Stressed, because they might be late.

10. Why didn't Michelle like some of the pieces of luggage?

    A They were cheap.

    B They were old and shabby.

    C They weren't hers.

    D They were embarrassing colours.

    E They were her parents'.

11. Why was Michelle concerned?

    A She thought that the luggage wouldn't fit in the car.

    B She thought they might be late.

    C She thought that her father would get into trouble with her mother.

    D She didn't want the neighbours to see the luggage.

    E She didn't think her mother would be ready in time.

12. What does paragraph eleven mostly suggest about Michelle's mother?

    A She is bossy.

    B She is a good cook.

    C She is able to multi-task.

    D She is skilful.

    E She is shrewd.

13. What does paragraph twelve mainly suggest about Mr and Mrs Wardle?

    A They are very similar characters.

    B Mrs Wardle resembles Mr Wardle.

    C Mrs Wardle is thoughtful and caring.

    D Mr Wardle and Mrs Wardle are analogous.

    E They are quite different characters.

14. What feeling does the paragraph beginning 'Michelle had been…' tell the reader about her?

    A She is apprehensive.

    B She is fitful.

    C She is quiet.

    D She is quietly excited.

    E She is nervous.

15. Why doesn't Michelle want to talk to her mother?

  A Her mother is boring.

  B She finds her annoying.

  C She knows that her mother isn't sensible.

  D She wants to concentrate on her book.

  E She wants to concentrate on the journey.

16. Which of these things doesn't happen to the car in the paragraph beginning 'There was a sound…'?

  A It explodes.

  B It breaks down.

  C It stops.

  D It makes a loud noise.

  E It leaks steam.

17. The writer says that Michelle looked at her 'dumbstruck mother' and her 'anxious father'. What does this mainly suggest about them at this point in the story?

  A They aren't very clever.

  B They don't know how to cope with what has happened to the car.

  C They were aghast at the scenery.

  D They were startled by their daughter.

  E They are confused.

18. What does the ending suggest?

  A The family will miss the plane.

  B The holiday will be delayed.

  C Michelle will sort out the problem.

  D Michelle's family will not get on with each other.

  E Mr and Mrs Wardle will get a taxi home.

Now answer the following questions about the meanings of these words and phrases as they are used in the story.

19. In paragraph one, the word 'peered' is used. Which of these is its closest meaning?

   A   yawned

   B   stared

   C   grabbed

   D   watched

   E   closed

20. The phrase 'fully co-ordinated' is used in the fourth paragraph. What does it mean?

   A   totally psyched-up

   B   totally observant

   C   wearing totally matching clothing

   D   totally disorganised

   E   in total shock

21. The phrase 'Michelle wasn't convinced that this advantage outweighed the embarrassment…' is used in paragraph eight. What does it mean?

   A   Michelle couldn't make her mind up.

   B   Michelle was embarrassed.

   C   Michelle thought that the suitcases were bad.

   D   Michelle didn't think that the advantage of being able to spot the cases made up for their brightness.

   E   Michelle couldn't have her mind changed.

22. The word 'tenderly' is used to describe how Michelle treated her father. Which of these is closest to its meaning?

   A   gently

   B   nervously

   C   roughly

   D   immediately

   E   sensibly

Now answer the following questions about words and phrases and how they are used in the passage.

23.   What type of words are these?

Michelle   Rome   Mr Wardle   Colosseum

A   Common nouns.

B   Verbs.

C   Adverbs.

D   Proper nouns.

E   Abstract nouns.

24.   'Michelle knew that he would accept.' Which of these words is a pronoun?

A   Michelle

B   accept

C   that

D   he

E   knew

25.   Which of these words is a common noun?

A   acknowledged

B   suitcases

C   designed

D   coming

E   peered

In the following passage there are some spelling mistakes. On each numbered line you will see that there is either one mistake or no mistake at all. Find the group of words with the mistake in it and mark its letter on your answer sheet. If there is no mistake, mark the letter N.

The Knight's Journey

26. Sir Godfrey road out of the castle, sitting proudly on his horse.

A	B	C	D

27. He was on a qwest to find the lost treasure of the ancients, which was

A	B	C	D

28. supposed to be hidden in the distant mountains. It was a legend and

A	B	C	D

29. no-one really new whether it existed or not – it was a puzzling mystery.

A	B	C	D

30. He had found an old scrole which had the treasure castle marked on

A	B	C	D

31. it, but no names of any places. Sir Godfrey was relaying on his own

A	B	C	D

32. knowledge of the mountains to try and work out where the castle

A	B	C	D

33. might be. On that day, he fealt that he was going to be successful.

A	B	C	D

In the following passage there are some mistakes to do with punctuation and capital letters. In each numbered line, you will find either one mistake or no mistake at all. Find the group of words with the mistake in it and mark its letter on your answer sheet. If there is no mistake, mark the letter N.

Lucie's Bike Ride

34. Lucie had received a new shiny bike for her birthday and she was anxious

    A   B   C   D

35. to try it out. she put on her safety helmet and sat astride the saddle.

    A   B   C   D

36. She had ridden a bike before, so why couldn't she do it again

    A   B   C   D

37. the first few yards were a bit wobbly but she kept going.

    A   B   C   D

38. Are you all right?" shouted her dad. He didn't want her to

    A   B   C   D

39. fall off and graze her knees like she had done before. "I'm fine,"

    A   B   C   D

40. replied Lucie. Unfortunately, in replying, she didn't watch where

    A   B   C   D

41. she was going and her front wheel caught the kerb – "Ouch" shouted Lucie.

    A   B   C   D

In the following questions you need to pick the most appropriate word or group of words so that the passage makes sense. Choose one of the five answers on each line and mark its letter on your answer sheet.

The Concert

42. Dave and his friends had put together a band to play

load	loud	louder	low	lode
A	B	C	D	E

music

43. because they

waited	warted	wanted	wailed	walked
A	B	C	D	E

to play at their year's prom.

44. Dave

deicided	defied	derided	decided	decried
A	B	C	D	E

to play the guitar and sing

45. and his cousin Stuart

brung	bought	brought	buyed	bringed
A	B	C	D	E

along his

drum kit.

46. They now

neaded	kneeled	needed	noticed	noted
A	B	C	D	E

a bass player who

47. could also learn

they're	there	they'res	there's	their
A	B	C	D	E

songs.

48. Stuart,

who's	whose	what's	which	whichever's
A	B	C	D	E

voice was good,

49. could also sing, but he

choose	chosen	choosed	chose	chosing
A	B	C	D	E

not to.

English
Multiple-Choice
Practice Test C

Read these instructions carefully:

1. You must not open or turn over this booklet until you are told to do so.

2. The booklet contains a passage for you to read and some questions for you to answer. You can refer to the passage to check your answers as many times as you want. You will then need to complete some spelling, punctuation and grammar exercises.

3. This is a multiple-choice test, so select your answers from the options on the answer sheet. Mark only **one** answer for each question.

4. Make sure you draw a line firmly through the rectangle next to your answer. If you make a mistake, rub it out as well as you can and mark your new answer.

5. Try to do as many questions as you can. If you find that you cannot do a question, do not waste time on it and simply go on to the next one. If you are stuck on a question, choose the answer that you think is best.

6. Do all rough working on a separate sheet of paper.

7. You have 50 minutes to complete the test.

Read the following passage carefully, then answer the questions.

The Story of Robin Hood

1 This story is hundreds of years old and has been passed down over generations by word of mouth and in many written versions. Different versions of the story are known in several parts of the United Kingdom and some places – especially in the Midlands and the North – claim to have a link with the story's hero. Even the name of the story's hero is not constant – but most people know him as Robin Hood.

2 The story begins around the time of the Crusades – Richard the Lionheart had left England and the country was being run by his brother, King John. King John used his brother Richard's absence to get his own way and run the country for his own wicked ends. Taxes were raised; the rich and the poor were thrown off their land and the ordinary man's right to hunt and farm was taken away. This great injustice caused incredible hardship. Anyone who sought to challenge the king's authority was hunted down and never seen again.

3 King John had spies up and down the land. He put his own men in positions of strength and influence all over the country to take away the land and property of anyone who might be powerful enough to challenge him. One such man was the Earl of Loxley, whose lands were taken from him. Not only that, but it was believed that he was imprisoned and put to death. His son, Robin, was sent away by the earl when he knew that he was in danger. He was brought up in secrecy, safely away from his father's former land, unaware of who his father was and what had happened to him.

4 Many years went by and the boy grew into a strong youth and, because he was obviously so unlike his elderly adoptive parents, he began to wonder who he really was. On his death bed, his guardian told Robin all. Distressed by the death of his father and overcome with rage at what had happened to his birth father, Robin vowed to find out who was responsible and take revenge.

5 Robin wasn't very careful about keeping his ideas secret at first and King John's spies found out that there was a young man intent on stirring up trouble. The man who was responsible for carrying out King John's orders in the area where Robin lived was called the Sheriff of Nottingham. He was particularly ruthless in carrying out the king's wishes and had many armed men and spies who would do his bidding.

6 It wasn't long, therefore, before the sheriff's men came looking for Robin. Luckily, Robin had been brought up amongst skilled woodsmen and he knew the ways of the forest and the places where the sheriff's men would never find him. At that time, forests were far bigger than they are now and Sherwood Forest was a dark and mysterious place where men could hide and, if they were careful, not get caught. Robin ran away from the sheriff's men and hid successfully in Sherwood Forest. At first, legend has it, he hid inside a massive oak tree with a hollow centre – the sheriff's men rode past and never suspected that he was inside.

7 In the days that followed, Robin discovered that he wasn't the only rebel taking refuge in the forests. One day, when attempting to cross a fierce stream along a fallen tree, he came face-to-face with a giant of a man. The tall man refused to move out of the way – and so did Robin. A challenge arose. Both men grabbed hold of large branches from the fallen tree and agreed to use them as weapons in the challenge that they had now set each other. The tall fellow swung for Robin first, but Robin was quick and nimble enough to dodge his attempted blow. Not only that, but as the giant of a man threw all his effort into his strike, Robin's dodge had set him off balance. Quick as a flash, Robin nudged him into the water, without the need for any great strength. Laughing, Robin gave his hand to the big, but rather wet giant, and helped him over to the side of the river. Fortunately, the soggy chap had enough good humour to see the funny side of what had happened to him! He shook Robin's hand and introduced himself as John Little – Robin quickly re-christened him Little John because of his great size. The two became firm friends almost immediately and Robin's band of outlaw brothers was born.

8 Many other men were soon to join Robin – men who had otherwise been of good character, but had been persecuted by the Sheriff of Nottingham and forced to take refuge in Sherwood Forest. Among them were men whose names, too, became part of the Robin Hood legend – Friar Tuck, Much the Miller, Will Scarlet and many others. Apart from Will Scarlet, who liked to wear reddish-brown clothing, Robin's men wore green clothing as a form of camouflage. This became known as Lincoln green.

9 Robin and his band of outlaws swore to fight back against the evil of the Sheriff of Nottingham and King John and help the poor of the land. They undertook many raids to help the poor and needy. On one such raid, Robin came across the beautiful Maid Marian, who, being of a caring and sensitive nature herself, sympathised with Robin's mission. She was upset by the evil doings that she saw going on in the name of the king, but felt powerless to do anything. She started to fall in love with Robin. The Sheriff of Nottingham realised this and hatched a secret plan to lure Robin into the open, where he could be captured. He organised an archery competition, with a golden arrow as its prize, to be presented by Maid Marian. Knowing that Robin would not resist the challenge, he surrounded the venue with thousands of his men, in disguise.

10 As the sheriff suspected, Robin did turn up, heavily disguised, at the tournament. After several rounds, there was only Robin and the sheriff's best archer left. The sheriff's man shot a perfect shot, exactly in the middle of the bullseye. The pressure was on, with Maid Marian and the sheriff watching and surrounded on all sides by the sheriff's men. But Robin came good – he shot his arrow and split the sheriff's man's arrow in two, winning the prize. As he went up to accept his golden arrow, the order was given to capture him – but Robin had out-thought the sheriff. Robin's men – also in disguise – leapt into the area where the sheriff and Maid Marian were seated and held the sheriff until Robin could get away with not only the golden arrow, but Maid Marian too…

11 This was one of many adventures that made Robin, Marian and their men into heroic figures. Eventually, King Richard escaped from his foreign prison and returned to England, where he knighted Robin for what he had done and returned the Earl of Loxley's land to its rightful owner – and also carried out the wedding of Robin and Marian!

Now answer these questions, looking at the passage again if you need to. Choose the most suitable answer in each case. Mark it on your answer sheet.

1. What is the main idea made in the first paragraph?

    A   The story of Robin Hood is varied.

    B   The story of Robin Hood is a recent one.

    C   The story of Robin Hood has many different sources and versions.

    D   The story of Robin Hood is about a hundred years old.

    E   The story of Robin Hood was never written down.

2. What is the purpose of the second paragraph?

    A   To give background to the story of Robin Hood.

    B   To divulge historical secrets about Robin.

    C   To give Robin's credentials.

    D   To explain who Robin's influences were.

    E   To describe Robin Hood.

3. In the second paragraph, the writer uses the words and phrases 'great injustice' and 'incredible hardship'. What is the likely effect of such phrases on the reader?

    A   To make the reader think that those times were hard for all people.

    B   To make the reader think that King John was laudable.

    C   To make the reader esteem Robin Hood.

    D   To make the reader sympathise with the situation of the people at that time.

    E   To make the reader feel sympathy towards the king.

4. What relation was the Earl of Loxley to Robin Hood?

    A   Uncle.

    B   Stepfather.

    C   Father-in-law.

    D   Son.

    E   Father.

5. In paragraph four, why did Robin become angry?

    A His adoptive father had been killed by King John.

    B His birth father had abandoned him as a baby.

    C He discovered the truth about his origins.

    D He had been punished by King John.

    E He had been lied to.

6. '…spies who would do his bidding…' – what is meant by this?

    A Spies who would do conspiratorial things.

    B Spies who would contravene the king's orders.

    C Spies who would do what they wanted.

    D Spies who would do what the sheriff wanted them to.

    E Spies who would do what Robin wanted them to.

7. Why was Robin's upbringing helpful?

    A He was able to fabricate armaments.

    B He could make things to help him contend with the sheriff.

    C He knew the ways of the forest, which helped him to evade capture.

    D He knew how to make bows and arrows.

    E He knew where the sheriff's men were.

8. Which of the following, according to the passage, was true about Sherwood Forest?

    1. It was dark and mysterious.

    2. It was very large.

    3. It had few roads.

    4. It had lots of resources.

    A 1 and 2

    B 1 and 3

    C 2 and 4

    D 2 and 3

    E 3 and 4

9. What did Robin and Little John both want to do, according to paragraph seven?

    A Have a fight.

    B Be friends.

    C Cross a river using the same crossing.

    D Make fun of each other.

    E Join a gang.

10. Why did Robin win the challenge between them?

    A He was tenacious and quicker.

    B He was diminutive and quicker.

    C He was more nimble and quicker.

    D He was more intelligent and quicker.

    E He was better prepared.

11. Who was the odd-one-out amongst Robin's men?

    A Robin

    B Little John

    C Friar Tuck

    D Will Scarlet

    E Much the Miller

12. Based on the whole text, which of these statements do you think reflects the writer's opinion?

    A Robin Hood was fortuitous in becoming famous.

    B Robin Hood was a felicitous warrior.

    C He sympathises with and likes Robin's deeds.

    D He doesn't have any strong like or dislike for Robin.

    E He is jealous of Robin.

13. What two things did the sheriff do to try and lure Robin to the archery competition?

    A He made a plan and disguised his men.

    B He used Maid Marian and a golden arrow as bait.

    C He obfuscated Robin.

    D He got Maid Marian and his men to be ready.

    E He contrived it so that Robin would win and had a recherché prize.

14. Which of these is not mentioned in the story?

    A Why the sheriff didn't like Robin.

    B What happened to Robin's birth father.

    C What happened to Robin's adoptive father.

    D How Friar Tuck joined the merry men.

    E How Maid Marian felt about Robin.

15. In the story of the archery competition, Robin pulled off a double-bluff. What was it?

    A He split an arrow in two.

    B He came in disguise.

    C He won Maid Marian and the arrow.

    D He tricked the sheriff by having his own men in disguise too.

    E He escaped.

16. In which of these would we be most likely to read this passage?

    A In a leaflet.

    B In a brochure.

    C In a children's reference book.

    D In an encyclopaedia.

    E In a newspaper.

17. In which paragraph does the writer first tell of Marian's feelings for Robin?

    A Paragraph six.

    B Paragraph seven.

    C Paragraph eight.

    D Paragraph nine.

    E Paragraph ten.

18. What main impression does the writer want to create with his final paragraph?

    A That Robin was a man who had England's true interests at heart.

    B That Robin was a fighter.

    C That Robin was in love with Marian.

    D That Robin only fought to earn rewards.

    E That Robin was in the right place at the right time.

Now answer the following questions about the meanings of words and phrases as they are used in the passage.

19. The text describes the sheriff as 'particularly ruthless'. What does this mean?

   A unkind

   B clever

   C very cruel

   D sneaky

   E suspicious

20. Which of these is closest to the meaning of 'challenge the king's authority' (paragraph two)?

   A Support the king.

   B Have a race with the king.

   C Surprise the king.

   D Go against the king.

   E Spy on the king.

21. In paragraph seven it says that Robin wasn't the only person 'taking refuge'. What does this mean?

   A Fighting against the sheriff.

   B Fighting against the king.

   C Raising an army.

   D Getting weapons.

   E Hiding away from danger.

22. Which of these phrases from the passage means 'a method of disguise'?

   A 'never suspected'

   B 'a form of camouflage'

   C 'reddish-brown clothing'

   D 'evil doings'

   E 'a secret plan'

Now answer the following questions about words and phrases from the passage.

23.   What type of words are these in the passage?

suspected   disguised   surrounded   returned

A   Nouns.

B   Adjectives.

C   Verbs.

D   Adverbs.

E   Prepositions.

24.   'This story is hundreds of years old…'

Which of these words is a verb?

A   story

B   is

C   hundreds

D   years

E   old

25.   'Robin could get away with not only the golden arrow, but Maid Marian too…'

What is the punctuation called at the end of this quotation?

A   Full stops.

B   Exclamation marks.

C   Hyphens.

D   Ellipsis.

E   Dashes.

In the following passage there are some spelling mistakes. On each numbered line you will see that there is either one mistake or no mistake at all. Find the group of words with the mistake in it and mark its letter on your answer sheet. If there is no mistake, mark the letter N.

The Big Match

26.   Bill had been wating for this day for a very long time indeed.

      A   B   C   D

27.   This was the day of the regional cup finnal, which his Sunday football

      A   B   C   D

28.   team had qualified for by winning a thrilling semi-final, after extra time

      A   B   C   D

29.   in near total darkness. There had been now floodlights at the venue where

      A   B   C   D

30.   the semi-final had taken plaice, but the teams had carried on into the

      A   B   C   D

31.   gathering glome. After both sides had failed to break the deadlock after extra time,

      A   B   C   D

32.   the game went to penalties. Bill had taken the desicive penalty and had scored,

      A   B   C   D

33.   sending his team into today's final – which would kick off in less then an hour…

      A   B   C   D

In the following passage there are some mistakes to do with punctuation and capital letters. In each numbered line, you will find either one mistake or no mistake at all. Find the group of words with the mistake in it and mark its letter on your answer sheet. If there is no mistake, mark the letter N.

Hide and Seek

34. Jenny had always wanted to play hide and seek in a forest. she was staying with her
    A   B   C   D

35. best friend, Emma, out in the countryside. her parents were out of the country on business,
    A   B   C   D

36. so she had two whole weeks to explore the deeply wooded hills near Emmas home. On
    A   B   C   D

37. the first morning of her stay, Jenny and Emma walked off into the dark damp and
    A   B   C   D

38. mysterious forest to play a game of hide and seek. Emma was the first to hide, but
    A   B   C   D

39. was quickly found by her friend. Jenny then hid. Emma shouted, "Coming? Ready or not!"
    A   B   C   D

40. and dashed into the darkness after jenny. The trees curled above, blocking the
    A   B   C   D

41. sky, but Emma felt safe and comfortable. "Where are you." she shouted.
    A   B   C   D

In the following passage, you need to pick the most appropriate word or group of words so that the passage makes sense. Choose one of the five answers on each line and mark its letter on your answer sheet.

The Secret

42. Deep in the jungles of | off | from | to | with Peru, there was a hidden
      A   B   C   D   E

43. temple witch | which | wish | what | with had lain undiscovered.
     A   B   C   D   E

44. It was unknown until the great explorer, Montana Smith
    disguised | decided | dismissed | discovered | disentangled it.
      A   B   C   D   E

45. It looked as | as like | as when | like | though no-one had seen it for
        A   B   C   D   E

46. centuries. Ivy and tree rots | rotes | routes | roots | rites covered it
        A   B   C   D   E

47. from top to bottom. Montana
    should have | should of | might of | could ought to have | did notified the
      A   B   C   D   E

    authorities, but he didn't want to.

48. The temple was different | unlike to | different from | unlike with | similar any others
          A   B   C   D   E

49. he had ever seen. He choose | choosed | chose | chosed | chosen to keep what he had
              A   B   C   D   E

    found secret.

English

Multiple-Choice
Practice Test D

Read these instructions carefully:

1. You must not open or turn over this booklet until you are told to do so.

2. The booklet contains a passage for you to read and some questions for you to answer. You can refer to the passage to check your answers as many times as you want. You will then need to complete some spelling, punctuation and grammar exercises.

3. This is a multiple-choice test, so select your answers from the options on the answer sheet. Mark only **one** answer for each question.

4. Make sure you draw a line firmly through the rectangle next to your answer. If you make a mistake, rub it out as well as you can and mark your new answer.

5. Try to do as many questions as you can. If you find that you cannot do a question, do not waste time on it and simply go on to the next one. If you are stuck on a question, choose the answer that you think is best.

6. Do all rough working on a separate sheet of paper.

7. You have 50 minutes to complete the test.

Read the following passage carefully, then answer the questions.

The Story of Ancient Rome

1   Rome, as a place, first seems to have developed in the 9th century BC, when an Iron Age settlement was established on what is now known as the Palatine Hill. It had no name until 753 BC, when the brothers Romulus and Remus – who, legend would have it, were raised by wolves – fought, and Romulus won. As a result, Romulus gave the newly formed city its name. Today, this legend is still in evidence all over the city.

2   Rome, at first, had kings and not emperors. Tarquinius Priscus was one of the first kings and his family ruled for over a century until 509 BC, when they were deposed and the people of the area created a republic.

3   Over the next few centuries, Rome grew, but also suffered many attacks from various European tribes. In 390 BC it was captured by the Gauls from what we now call France. Shortly after this, a huge wall was built around the city to try and protect it from attack. This didn't stop many forces trying to attack though, as they would do for many centuries afterwards.

4   The next centuries were unsettled – in 73 BC there was a slave revolt headed by a man named Spartacus, whose story was made into a largely fictitious film, nearly 2000 years later! In the years between 65 and 60 BC, a man appeared whose name has come to be associated with the growth of the Roman Empire – Julius Caesar. He won many important battles and held many high-ranking posts in the Roman system of government. At first, Julius Caesar jointly ruled Rome with Crassus and Pompey, but after a successful invasion and colonisation of Gaul (France) he returned and crossed the Rubicon river. There, Julius Caesar started a civil war with Pompey, which Caesar finally won.

5   His victory did not last, however, and in 44 BC Julius Caesar was assassinated. Once again, Rome had a period when it had many different leaders – Antony, Augustus, Caligula, Claudius and Nero all achieved different reputations, not all of them good, especially in the case of Caligula and Nero. The phrase 'fiddle while Rome burns' – meaning someone who stands by and does nothing when something bad is happening – was supposed to have been based on the behaviour of the Emperor Nero after a huge city-wide fire in 64 AD.

6   It wasn't until 69 AD and the Emperor Vespasian that order returned to the city of Rome. Vespasian built the famous Colosseum, which still stands today. Trajan became Emperor in 98 AD and ruled over one of the most stable times in Roman history up until this point. He was followed by Hadrian – famous for giving his name to the wall that divides England and Scotland, but he did far more than this and he expanded the Roman Empire, increasing its wealth and power. Members of the Roman Army no longer came from just Rome – archaeological evidence shows that soldiers serving Rome came from all over Europe and North Africa. Quite what men originally from warmer Mediterranean countries thought of having to serve in the cold south

of Scotland is not fully known, but from what little evidence we have, it seems as though it wasn't the most popular posting for a Roman soldier!

7   For the next couple of hundred years, Rome's power and lands grew, but its golden age was probably over. In 306, Constantine became the empire's first Christian emperor. He also moved the centre of the empire away from Rome, to a city then called Byzantium, now known as Istanbul. Rome's empire was becoming too large and very difficult to control, however, and it was difficult for the emperor and his system of government to keep control over lands that were so far away. In 410, the Roman Empire suffered a huge blow, when the city of Rome was captured by a tribe called the Visigoths. This was the first time that the city had been captured by foreign forces in over 800 years, and it was a clear sign that Rome was no longer the power that it once had been. Over the next 100 years, the city was attacked again and its population fell to around 30,000 – it had been a city of over a million in its heyday.

8   After this time, the story of Rome changes from one of rival emperors and tribes to one of rival families, countries and beliefs. The Rome that lives long in our imagination, however, has survived remarkably well into the modern age. Anyone who visits Rome today will still see many features of ancient times, some untouched, some changed and some still being uncovered.

9   The Pantheon, a massive dome-like building which later became a church, gives us some idea of the scale of the buildings in ancient times. Compared to what existed in most of Western Europe at that time, buildings like the Pantheon must surely have amazed ancient visitors. The Colosseum, which is the size of a modern sports stadium – and the model for most stadiums in the world today – has had a great deal of its stone taken away, but still stands as a Roman icon. Next door to the Colosseum is the Roman Forum, where the main buildings, like the Senate, important temples and the homes of some of the emperors could be found. In the 17th and 18th centuries it was believed to be essential, as part of the education of a wealthy young man, to travel Europe and do a trip called 'The Grand Tour' in order to see these wonders of the ancient world. Even after nearly one and a half thousand years, people were still in awe of the achievements of the ancient Romans.

10 As you walk around modern-day Rome, it is still easy to see parts of the ancient city all around you – a part of a wall here, a broken statue there – all merged into the modern-day Roman world. As new buildings are created, more digging takes place and even more secrets of the ancient world are revealed. Such is the care that has to be taken when building in Rome, so as not to disturb and destroy the past, that new developments take place quite slowly. When time and care are taken, however, the stories that are revealed to us bring to life the past in many fascinating ways.

11 Although ancient Rome's golden age was over by the 4th century AD, it is still affecting the lives of modern-day Romans and millions of tourists every year. Who knows what still lies beneath the streets and who knows what we will learn about the ancient past, at some time in the future?

Now answer these questions, looking at the passage again if you need to. Choose the most suitable answer in each case. Mark it on your answer sheet.

1. When did Rome first develop as a place?

    A   In the Bronze Age.

    B   On the Palatine hill.

    C   In the 9th century AD.

    D   In the 9th century BC.

    E   In Italy.

2. How did Rome get its name?

    A   It was named after a hill.

    B   It was named after a river.

    C   It was named after Romulus.

    D   It was named after Remus.

    E   It was named after a wolf.

3. What was Rome ruled by before it became a republic?

    A   A king.

    B   An emperor.

    C   A queen.

    D   A prince.

    E   A regent.

4. Why was a wall built around Rome?

    A   To keep the Gauls in.

    B   To help the forces outside Rome.

    C   To show the border of Rome.

    D   To protect Rome.

    E   To capture attackers.

5. Why is Spartacus famous?

    A He was in a film.

    B He was a slave.

    C He told stories.

    D He spearheaded a revolt.

    E He ruled Rome.

6. Which of these is not a factor which helped Julius to become emperor?

    A He won many salient battles.

    B He colonised Gaul.

    C He held many high-ranking posts in Roman society.

    D He spent time away from Rome.

    E He was a joint ruler before he became sole ruler.

7. Which of these men did not rule after Julius Caesar?

    A Pompey

    B Nero

    C Trajan

    D Caligula

    E Claudius

8. According to the passage, why did Nero get a bad reputation?

    A He was an unsatisfactory virtuoso.

    B He set fire to Roman enclaves.

    C He stood by and did nothing while Rome burnt.

    D He wasn't good at putting out fires.

    E He was friends with Caligula.

9. What does the passage imply Vespasian is most famous for?

    A Ruling Rome.

    B Building the Colosseum.

    C Giving orders.

    D Being emperor.

    E Ruling before Hadrian.

10. Why was Hadrian important?

   A He built a wall dividing England and Scotland.

   B He expanded the Roman Empire.

   C He increased the Empire's wealth.

   D Answers A, B and C.

   E Answers A and C.

11. According to the passage, why wasn't a posting to Hadrian's Wall likely to be popular for Roman soldiers?

   A There was no entertainment.

   B The Scots were troublesome.

   C It was cold.

   D It was dark.

   E The locals weren't friendly.

12. How do we know from the passage that Roman soldiers came from more places than just Rome?

   A Archaeological evidence tells us.

   B Historians tell us.

   C Annalists tell us.

   D Recent historiographic sources tell us.

   E English books tell us.

13. Why was the Roman Empire having problems in the 4th century?

   A It had a different centre.

   B It had a new emperor.

   C It was becoming too large to run.

   D It was getting smaller.

   E Its best days were over.

14. What did the invasion of the Visigoths demonstrate?

   A That Rome's power had weakened.

   B That Rome had no army.

   C That all Rome's soldiers were somewhere else.

   D That the Visigoths knew the Roman ingress.

   E That Rome's denizens had decreased in number.

15. How much of Ancient Rome has survived, according to the information in the passage?

   A   Nothing at all.

   B   Only a few buildings like the Colosseum and the Pantheon.

   C   Quite a lot.

   D   All of it.

   E   Just the Colosseum, the Pantheon and the Forum.

16. According to the passage, how has the Colosseum influenced modern buildings?

   A   Its vast size inspired modern skyscrapers.

   B   It was built from stone.

   C   It was built to last.

   D   Its design influenced modern stadiums.

   E   Its iconic design inspires modern architecture.

17. What was 'The Grand Tour'?

   A   A peregrination around Rome.

   B   A Roman ritual.

   C   Part of the education of wealthy young men in the past.

   D   A very expensive pilgrimage.

   E   A pleasure break.

18. What does the writer think about the secrets of Ancient Rome?

   A   They have been thoroughly disclosed.

   B   Many of them have been eradicated.

   C   They will never be unearthed.

   D   There are more still to be revealed.

   E   They shouldn't be disturbed.

Now answer the following questions about the meanings of these words and phrases as they are used in the story.

19. In paragraph two, what does 'deposed' mean?

   A testified

   B removed from power

   C designated

   D put in charge

   E unmodified

20. What does 'fictitious' mean in paragraph four?

   A real

   B famous

   C interesting

   D historical

   E made up

21. What does 'golden age' in paragraph seven mean?

   A best times

   B treasure

   C duration

   D century

   E worst times

22. What does 'merged' mean in paragraph ten?

   A built

   B constructed

   C broken

   D mixed in with

   E apart from

Now answer the following questions about words and phrases and how they are used in the passage.

23. What types of words are these?

Pantheon   Rome   Colosseum   Vespasian

   A   Common nouns.

   B   Adverbs.

   C   Abstract nouns.

   D   Proper nouns.

   E   Adjectives.

24. 'Over the next few centuries, Rome grew…' Which of these words is a verb?

   A   Over

   B   centuries

   C   Rome

   D   next

   E   grew

25. '**Rome**, at first, had **kings** and not **emperors**.' Which of these describes the words that are in **bold** type?

   A   Nouns.

   B   Prepositions.

   C   Clauses.

   D   Verbs.

   E   Adjectives.

In the following passage there are some spelling mistakes. On each numbered line you will see that there is either one mistake or no mistake at all. Find the group of words with the mistake in it and mark its letter on your answer sheet. If there is no mistake, mark the letter N.

The Sea Journey

26. Many years ago, a ship's captin sailed in search of new lands far away
     A · · · · · · B · · · · · · C · · · · · · D

27. across the sea. He knew that their would be many dangers to face and
     A · · · · · · B · · · · · · C · · · · · · D

28. many problems too conquer. His crew consisted of men who had served
     A · · · · · · B · · · · · · C · · · · · · D

29. him well on many previous voyages. They where all brave, courageous and bold and
     A · · · · · · B · · · · · · C · · · · · · D

30. not easily scared. However, nothing could have easily prepared them for what
     A · · · · · · B · · · · · · C · · · · · · D

31. they were about to encounter on this fated voyage. Three short daze into
     A · · · · · · B · · · · · · C · · · · · · D

32. the jurney, the look-out spotted a dark shape on the horizon. As they
     A · · · · · · B · · · · · · C · · · · · · D

33. sailed closer, it turned out to be a gigantic see creature they had never seen before.
     A · · · · · · B · · · · · · C · · · · · · D

In the following passage there are some mistakes to do with punctuation and capital letters. In each numbered line, you will find either one mistake or no mistake at all. Find the group of words with the mistake in it and mark its letter on your answer sheet. If there is no mistake, mark the letter N.

The First Day

34. on your first day at a new school, there are lots of things that might

    A   B   C   D

35. go wrong. You might catch the wrong bus and arrive late turn up at

    A   B   C   D

36. the wrong school or even forget to switch on the alarm clock and over-sleep.

    A   B   C   D

37. Wearing the wrong uniform would be a bad thing to do. "why are you

    A   B   C   D

38. wearing that purple tie, young lady? would be the question. That would

    A   B   C   D

39. be difficult to answer if your own schools tie was green or red.

    A   B   C   D

40. it would be even more embarrassing if you joined the wrong class and spent

    A   B   C   D

41. the day with people in a different younger age group.

    A   B   C   D

In the following section, you need to pick the most appropriate word or group of words so that the passage makes sense. Choose one of the five answers on each line and mark its letter on your answer sheet.

The Spooky House

42.   One day, Jenny and Craig decided | too | to | that | was | which | visit the
                                          A   B   C   D   E

43.   old house on the corner of | there | they're | those | their | there's | street.
                                     A   B   C   D   E

44.   It stood tall, dark and alone, | which | but | otherwise | because | when | it had been
                                         A   B   C   D   E

      empty for years,

45.   abandoned by | their | its | it's | there | theirs | owners. Craig
                       A   B   C   D   E

46. | would | shouldn't | hadn't | couldn't | did | understand why no-one
         A   B   C   D   E

47.   had visited it before. It looked scarier in the dark, | because | which | from | thus | then
                                                                 A   B   C   D   E

48.   moonlight cast a strange glow over it. | This | That | Them | That's | They's | why
                                                 A   B   C   D   E

49.   Craig decided that to visit at night would be the | best | better | good | well | goodly | time.
                                                            A   B   C   D   E

PRACTICE PAPERS

Answers and Explanations

English

Practice Test A Answers and Explanations

1. **B**
The story is told in the third person so it's not told *by* a pirate (A). There is no mention of a pet (D) and it hasn't been made up (C) as there are historical references.

2. **D**
France and Spain owned land surrounding the 'Neutral Strip' but clearly neither owned it individually or jointly. We know from paragraph one that Jean Lafitte was one of many who fought over American land, so he didn't own it either.

3. **C**
The text says 'difficult to navigate' and 'very hot and uncomfortable' in paragraph two.

4. **A**
We are told this in paragraph three and also that he would 'sell his slaves' to plantation owners in Louisiana.

5. **C**
In paragraph four we learn that other pirates, allies of Jean Lafitte, set up their own bases. These had a 'positive impact' in that the few locals who lived in the swamps were able to get across the rivers and use the trading posts.

6. **E**
In paragraph five we are told 'the legend of Jean Lafitte started to grow' and 'an air of mystery' about him was created, as people spread tales about where he kept his riches.

7. **B**
Jean Lafitte gave expensive gifts, to keep the people on his side (see paragraph six), despite sometimes stealing them back again.

8. **C**
Paragraph eight explains that although the plan was for Lafitte to meet Napoleon and his treasure in Bordeaux and then escape to Louisiana, Napoleon didn't show up so Lafitte sailed away with just the treasure.

9. **D**
Paragraph nine tells us that Napoleon's men received a particularly 'warm welcome' if they brought supplies with them to Louisiana.

10. **A**
The stories are difficult to prove because 'men feared for their lives' if they told what they knew about Jean Lafitte.

11. **B**
We know the men came to Contraband Bayou to search for treasure so the 'strange instruments' were clearly connected to this. After taking measurements with these instruments, they rode off into the swamps and returned with treasures (paragraph eleven).

12. **C**
One of Catalon's friends found a hole in the ground containing a skeleton of a 'sea-going man'. The suggestion is made that the treasure had been there due to him having a 'shovel in his hand' (paragraph twelve).

13. **D**
Catalon knew from his friend what had happened to someone else who knew too much about the treasure (see previous question) and although Catalon obviously knew a lot about the hidden treasure, and

might have wanted to reveal where it was, he would have been scared about the consequences (paragraph thirteen).

14. **C**
A is mentioned in paragraph fifteen: 'there is often a mysterious glow around the place where the gold is supposed to be hidden...'; B is mentioned in same paragraph; D is mentioned in same paragraph; E is mentioned in paragraph ten.

15. **B**
None of the others are hinted at in the text. The author says it is hard to know what to believe because of the terrain (paragraph seventeen 'the swamp is still large' and guarded by alligators) and in paragraph thirteen he says Lafitte 'didn't leave any written down stories behind, only rumours and handed-down hints', thus a lack of historical evidence.

16. **C**
There is too much information for A to be correct; a dictionary (B) would be clearly inappropriate; there is too much information for D (encyclopaedia) to be correct as well as not enough accurate facts due to lack of evidence; E would not be impossible but the story format would have to be dramatically changed and reduced as comics tend to be short and visual with very little text.

17. **A**
In paragraph sixteen we are told that Lafitte has streets and a National Park named after him.

18. **D**
The writer suggests there might be some 'left-over gold' (A); he refers to the swamp being 'still large' (B); he infers the swamps are dangerous by saying 'alligators still guard their territory' (C) and he implies that any remaining treasure – 'Lafitte's secrets' – might not be found for a while (E).

19. **B**
Although 'take refuge' can mean 'take shelter', in this context the writer was meaning that 'lawless men' would hide from the law.

20. **A**
Persecution usually does mean being badly treated for one reason or another, e.g. it can refer to religious prejudice where people are unfairly treated because of their religion.

21. **E**
'Escapade' means something that involves excitement, daring or adventure, which certainly applies to Lafitte.

22. **C**
'Romanticised' means something has been made to seem better or more appealing than it really is. Although what Lafitte did was against the law, his reputation is also that of a man who would help others and thus the illegal aspect of his way of life was somewhat overlooked.

23. **D**
Nouns are naming words of things, people and animals. They also name things we cannot see or touch, such as profit.

24. **B**
Catalon is a proper noun (A), age is a noun (C), old is an adjective (D) and to is a preposition (E).

54

25. C

A proverb (A) is a popular saying, 'Did he know where the treasure was?' is not a joke (B), a summary (D) or a title (E). As the word 'question' appears in the answer C, and there is a question mark at the end of the sentence, then clearly it is a question. It is a rhetorical question because an answer is not expected to be given.

26. D

The misspelt word in the group is 'grate', which should be 'great'.

27. D

The misspelt word in the group is 'their', which should be 'there'.

28. N

There are no spelling mistakes.

29. C

The misspelt word in the group is 'distance', which should be 'distant'.

30. B

The misspelt word in the group is 'hoarse', which should be 'horse'.

31. A

The misspelt word in the group is 'shon', which should be 'shone'.

32. N

There are no spelling mistakes.

33. D

The misspelt word in the group is 'pane', which should be 'pain'.

34. C

There is a capital letter missing from 'he' at the start of this group of words:
He didn't have enough

35. D

There are a comma and inverted commas missing from this group of words:
She said, "I'm

36. N

There are no errors.

37. A

There is a full stop missing from the end of this group of words:
to his bedroom.

38. N

There are no errors.

39. C

The full stop should be a comma and so the S should not be a capital letter:
and done with, so

40. A

There shouldn't be a capital letter at the start of this group of words:
be spending the

41. D

There should be a question mark at the end of this group of words:
What was it?

42. A

This is the correct verb form for the subject, 'she'. None of the others make sense.

43. C

This is the correct verb form for the subject, 'she'. None of the others make sense.

44. B

This is the correct verb form for the subject, 'she'. None of the others make sense.

45. D

This is the correct verb form for the subject, 'painting'. None of the others make sense.

46. B

No other conjunction makes sense.

47. A

No other word makes sense.

48. C

No other preposition makes sense.

49. A

No other verb form makes sense. Flews isn't a real word.

Practice Test B Answers and Explanations

1. **B**
   The writer tells us explicitly in paragraph one that 'it was still dark'.

2. **D**
   This is the most likely answer as none of the others make sense, but the writer implies that rubbing her eyes will help her see the clock better.

3. **E**
   The writer tells us explicitly in paragraph two that this was the first time that Michelle had been abroad AND her first time on a plane.

4. **C**
   We know that Michelle's mother is downstairs because in paragraph three we are told that 'Michelle's mother acknowledged her from the kitchen' and previously we are told that a voice calls up from below, which we can now assume is her mother's.

5. **B**
   We know from paragraph four that Michelle is a well-organised person – 'she'd sensibly left her travelling clothes out, ready for a quick getaway'.

6. **D**
   Michelle's mother tells her in paragraph five that she thinks her father needs some help carrying the cases to the car. None of the other answers apply.

7. **D**
   We already know that Michelle is well-organised (question 5). The writer implies that Michelle's father isn't very well-organised because he needs help to carry the cases to the car. Furthermore, we are told about his 'absent-minded quirkiness', which gives the impression of someone slightly scatty.

8. **E**
   Michelle makes suggestions to her father about where he might put the cases. She doesn't take over – she treats him 'tenderly'.

9. **B**
   Although Michelle is helpful, she does not imply that her father isn't very clever. She is caring because she knows he probably got up before 5 a.m. and thinks he needs to be 'treated tenderly' (paragraph nine).

10. **D**
    In paragraph eight the writer describes the vivid colours and patterns of the suitcases which Michelle's mother had bought so they would be easily spotted on the carousel. However, Michelle believed that her embarrassment at being seen with such cases would be far worse than not being able to spot them.

11. **D**
    Michelle was relieved that the leopard-print case, which she found embarrassing, had been put at the bottom of the luggage pile and was thus not visible to any neighbours who might be looking out of their windows (paragraph ten).

12. **C**
    Michelle's mother has not only sorted out food for the journey to the airport, she has put them into carrier bags and whilst holding the bags, locks the front door with her 'few free fingers'. She's not stressed because she calls 'cheerily', giving the impression that she's totally in control.

13. **E**
    The two parents are quite different: Mr Wardle is 'gracious with his compliments' which refers back to the last line of paragraph eleven when he told Mrs Wardle that Michelle had helped him. Mrs Wardle is firing questions at him which he answers in a very laid-back way, with the implication that he may not have done any of the jobs she is asking about because he was 'paying no attention at all'. Mrs Wardle seems organised and Mr Wardle seems scatty.

14. **D**
    The reader can tell that Michelle is quietly excited because the writer says she 'had been looking forward to this holiday for months'. The writer doesn't say she was worried or jumping up and down in her seat. She is excited at being able to see first-hand the places she has loved studying in school.

15. **D**
    Michelle doesn't want to talk to her mother because she wants to read her book – we are told this explicitly in paragraph fourteen.

16. **A**
    There is no indication whatsoever that the car explodes in paragraph sixteen but it does stop, it does break down, it does make a loud noise and it does leak steam.

17. **B**
    This is the most obvious answer; the description of Michelle's parents as dumb-struck and anxious tells us that they aren't confident about being able to deal with a breakdown. We are not told that they aren't clever, we are told nothing about the scenery, they aren't confused about anything and Michelle has been sitting quietly in the back.

18. **C**
    The writer implies that Michelle might be rummaging in her jeans pocket for her mobile phone to call for 'an emergency taxi' and sort out their problem.

19. **B**
    No other word makes sense.

20. **C**
    No other phrase makes sense. Co-ordinated clothing is clothing that matches, either in the sense of colour and/or similar material.

21. **D**
    Michelle didn't think that the ability to spot their cases on the carousel because of their brightness was worth the embarrassment of being seen to be the owner of such suitcases.

22. **A**
    No other word makes sense.

23. **D**
    Proper nouns always start with a capital. They name people and places.

24. **D**
    'He' is the only pronoun in the selection. A is a proper noun, B is a verb, C is a relative pronoun and E is a verb.

25. **B**
    'Suitcases' is a common noun but the rest are verbs.

26. **A**
    The misspelt word in the group is 'road', which should be 'rode'.

27. **A**

The misspelt word in the group is 'qwest', which should be 'quest'.

28. **N**

There are no misspelt words.

29. **B**

The misspelt word in the group is 'new', which should be 'knew'.

30. **B**

The misspelt word in the group is 'scrole', which should be 'scroll'.

31. **D**

The misspelt word in the group is 'relaying', which should be 'relying'.

32. **N**

There are no misspelt words.

33. **C**

The misspelt word in the group is 'fealt', which should be 'felt'.

34. **B**

There should be a comma between 'new' and 'shiny'.

35. **B**

The word 'she' should start with a capital letter because it's the beginning of the sentence.

36. **D**

There should be a question mark after 'again' at the end of this group of words because it's a question.

37. **A**

The word 'the' should start with a capital letter because it's the beginning of a sentence.

38. **A**

There should be inverted commas before the word 'Are' at the start of the speech.

39. **D**

There is an apostrophe missing between 'I' and 'm' in the word 'I'm'.

40. **B**

There should be a comma after the adverb, 'Unfortunately,'.

41. **D**

There should be an exclamation mark after the word 'Ouch!' as it's a cry of pain.

42. **B**

'Loud' is the most sensible word in the context – low music would not normally be associated with a prom. The other words don't make sense.

43. **C**

'Wanted' is the only verb that makes sense.

44. **D**

'Decided' is the only verb that makes sense.

45. **C**

'Brought' is the grammatically correct verb form of 'bring'. 'Brought' has a different meaning.

46. **C**

'Needed' is the only verb that makes sense.

47. **E**

'Their' is grammatically correct. It is the possessive article linked to 'songs'.

48. **B**

'Whose' is correct because it is the relative pronoun referring to Stuart's voice.

49. **D**

'Chose' is the only verb that makes sense.

Practice Test C Answers and Explanations

1. **C**
The writer states quite clearly that the story of Robin Hood has many different versions and sources: 'passed down over generations by word of mouth and in many written versions'.

2. **A**
The second paragraph doesn't describe Robin Hood, give his credentials or tell us who his influences were. Neither does it give historical secrets about him. The writer tells us about the Crusades that were happening at the time and how taxes were increased.

3. **D**
There are no other answers that make sense. Answer A is similar but does not include the idea of sympathy, which is what the writer wants the reader to feel.

4. **E**
The writer tells the reader explicitly in paragraph three that Loxley was Robin's father: '...the Earl of Loxley... put to death. His son, Robin, was...'

5. **C**
None of the other answers are true. His adoptive parents hadn't told him the truth up to that point but neither had they lied to him. Robin was angry to hear about how his father might have died.

6. **D**
The phrase 'do his bidding' means 'do what someone is asking of you'. The correct answer is D – 'his' refers to the sheriff.

7. **C**
Robin had been 'brought up amongst skilled woodsmen and he knew the ways of the forest and the places the sheriff's men would never find him' – this would help him avoid being captured.

8. **A**
Sherwood Forest was dark, mysterious and very large. The answer could only be 1. and 2. because neither 3. nor 4. are stated.

9. **C**
The writer tells us explicitly in paragraph seven that when he was 'attempting to cross a fierce stream along a fallen tree', Robin met a tall man who later turned out to be Little John. The implication is that he too was trying to cross the stream.

10. **C**
The writer tells the reader explicitly in paragraph seven that Robin was 'quick and nimble'.

11. **D**
In paragraph eight we learn that Will Scarlet was the only one who didn't wear camouflaged green clothing.

12. **C**
The writer doesn't say anything negative about Robin Hood's deeds and generally shows that he sympathises with him. He paints a positive picture of him.

13. **B**
The writer tells us in paragraph nine that the sheriff organised the archery competition as a way to lure Robin into the open, knowing he wouldn't be able to resist the prize of a golden arrow presented by the beautiful Maid Marian.

14. **D**
The writer mentions the other four in the story but nowhere is there a reference to how Friar Tuck joined the merry men. The only reference to him is in paragraph eight.

15. **D**
A double-bluff is a clever trick where one person deceives the person who believes they are the deceiver, in the way that Robin did by disguising his own men as the sheriff disguised his.

16. **C**
There is too much text to be appropriate for a leaflet or a brochure, where text is usually in sections with sub-headings and pictures; encyclopaedias and newspapers provide factual information, whereas this is a story.

17. **D**
In paragraph nine, the writer says that Marian 'started to fall in love with Robin'.

18. **A**
None of the other options are mentioned, although we do learn that Robin and Marian got married. Robin would not have been knighted by King Richard if he hadn't served his country well.

19. **C**
'Particularly ruthless' can only mean 'very cruel'. A ('unkind') is not strong enough and the other options mean something quite different.

20. **D**
'To challenge someone' means to go up against them; support (A) is the opposite of challenge, and the other answers are equally incorrect.

21. **E**
'Taking refuge' can mean 'taking shelter' but in this context it is 'hiding away from danger'.

22. **B**
'Camouflage' means being able to blend in to the background and thereby be barely seen, as if in disguise.

23. **C**
No other answer is correct. Nouns are naming words for things, people and places; adjectives describe nouns; adverbs describe a verb and prepositions are words that tell us the relationship between a noun or pronoun and another word in the sentence.

24. **B**
'Is' comes from the verb 'to be'.

25. **D**
Three dots at the end of a sentence is called an ellipsis.

26. **B**
The misspelt word in the group is 'wating', which should be 'waiting'.

27. **C**
The misspelt word in the group is 'finnal', which should be 'final'.

28. **N**
There are no misspelt words in any of the groups.

29. **C**
The misspelt word in the group is 'now', which should be 'no'.

30. **B**
The misspelt word in the group is 'plaice', which should be 'place'.

31. **A**
The misspelt word in the group is 'glome' which should be 'gloom'.

32. **C**

The misspelt word in the group is 'desicive' which should be 'decisive'.

33. **D**

The misspelt word in the group is 'then' which should be 'than'.

34. **D**

The word 'she' should start with a capital letter because it is the start of a new sentence.

35. **B**

The word 'her' should start with a capital letter because it is the start of a new sentence.

36. **D**

The word 'Emmas' should be written with an apostrophe to show possession because it is 'Emma's home'.

37. **D**

There is a comma missing between 'dark' and 'damp'.

38. **N**

There are no mistakes in any of these groups.

39. **C**

There should not be a question mark after 'Coming?' There should be an exclamation mark.

40. **B**

The word 'jenny' should start with a capital letter because 'Jenny' is a proper noun.

41. **C**

There should be a question mark instead of a full stop after "Where are you."

42. **A**

No other word is correct.

43. **B**

'Which' is the correct relative pronoun referring back to 'temple'. 'Wish' and 'witch' are nouns and therefore would not make sense at all. 'What' and 'with' do not make sense.

44. **D**

None of the other verbs make sense.

45. **D**

The other options do not make sense.

46. **D**

'Routes' is a homophone for 'roots' but means 'paths or roads'. The other words do not make sense.

47. **A**

'Should have' is the correct verb form. The others are incorrect.

48. **C**

'Different from' is the correct adjectival phrase in this context. The other options do not make sense.

49. **C**

'Chose' is the only verb form from the verb 'to choose' that makes sense.

Practice Test D Answers and Explanations

1. **D**
    Straightforward recall from text – paragraph one.

2. **C**
    Paragraph one tells us 'Romulus gave the newly formed city its name.'

3. **A**
    Rome was ruled by kings until they were deposed by the people of the area, who created the republic (paragraph two).

4. **D**
    Paragraph three tells us explicitly that a wall was built around Rome to 'protect it from attack'.

5. **D**
    The fact that he was in a film was only because he was famous for spearheading a revolt.

6. **D**
    All the other answers are true (see paragraph four) but time spent away from Rome is not explicitly mentioned.

7. **A**
    All the other men are mentioned as rulers who came after Julius Caesar. Pompey ruled Rome alongside Caesar and Crassus (paragraph four).

8. **C**
    Paragraph five reveals that it is thought Nero stood by and did nothing while Rome burnt. There is no reference to any of the other answers.

9. **B**
    Paragraph six tells us explicitly that 'Vespasian built the famous Colosseum'. Although he was an emperor, the implication is that he is remembered more for the Colosseum 'which still stands today'.

10. **D**
    He did all three things referred to in A, B and C as outlined in paragraph six.

11. **C**
    In paragraph six, the writer wonders what men from warm countries must have thought about coming to 'serve in the cold south of Scotland', then goes on to say 'it seems as though it wasn't the most popular posting for a Roman soldier!'

12. **A**
    Paragraph six tells us 'archaeological evidence shows that soldiers serving Rome came from all over Europe and North Africa'.

13. **C**
    Paragraph seven explains that Rome in the 4th century 'was becoming too large and very difficult to control.'

14. **A**
    The invasion of the Visigoths showed that 'Rome was no longer the power that it once had been' (paragraph seven), meaning its power had weakened.

15. **C**
    In paragraph eight the writer tells us that Rome has 'survived remarkably well into the modern age', which implies 'quite a lot'. Furthermore, he tells us that visitors to Rome will still see 'many features of ancient times'.

16. **D**
    In paragraph nine, the writer says that the Colosseum is 'the model for most stadiums in the world today.'

17. **C**
    In the past, young men travelled to Europe to see the wonders of the ancient world – this was called 'The Grand Tour' (see paragraph nine).

18. **D**
    In paragraph ten the writer says that 'even more secrets of the ancient are revealed' as more digging takes place.

19. **B**
    'Deposed' means removed from power. None of the other answers would make sense.

20. **E**
    'Fictitious' means made up, in the same way that fiction writing, or story writing, is made up.

21. **A**
    None of the other answers make sense. Gold is usually associated with glamour so 'golden age' is going to have a positive meaning.

22. **D**
    No other answer makes sense. 'Merging' things together means putting them together or mixing them in.

23. **D**
    Proper nouns always start with a capital. They name people and places.

24. **E**
    A verb is a 'doing' word; none of the other answers are verbs.

25. **A**
    All three are nouns – nouns are naming words for people, places and things.

26. **B**
    The misspelt word is 'captin', which should be spelled 'captain'.

27. **B**
    The misspelt word is 'their', which should be spelled 'there'.

28. **A**
    The misspelt word is 'too', which should be spelled 'to'.

29. **C**
    The misspelt word is 'where', which should be spelled 'were'.

30. **N**
    There are no misspelt words in these groups.

31. **D**
    The misspelt word is 'daze', which should be spelled 'days'.

32. **A**
    The misspelt word is 'jurney', which should be spelled 'journey'.

33. **C**
    The misspelt word is 'see', which should be spelled 'sea'.

34. **A**
    The word 'on' should start with a capital letter, as it is the start of a sentence.

35. **D**
    There should be a comma after the word 'late', as the writer is listing the various things that could go wrong.

36. **A**
    There should be a comma after the word 'school'.

37. **D**
    The word 'why' should start with a capital letter because it is the start of direct speech.

38. B
   There should be inverted commas after the question mark to indicate the end of direct speech.
39. C
   There should be an apostrophe after the letter l in the word 'schools' to indicate possession: 'the school's tie'.
40. A
   The word 'it' should start with a capital letter because it is the start of a sentence.
41 C
   There should be a comma between the words 'different' and 'younger'.
42. B
   No other word or spelling makes sense. The word 'too' means 'as well' or the idea of having 'too much' of something.
43. D
   'Their' is the possessive pronoun indicating the street 'belonging' to Jenny and Craig.
44. D
   'Because' is a conjunction introducing the subordinate clause which tells us why the house was tall, dark and alone.
45. B
   'Its' is the possessive pronoun referring to the house's owners. 'It's' means 'it is' so that wouldn't make sense.
46. D
   No other word(s) makes sense.
47. A
   'Because' is a conjunction introducing the subordinate clause which tells us why the house was scarier in the dark.
48. D
   No other answer makes sense.
49. A
   No other answer makes sense.

Notes

Notes

Notes

Pupil's Name

School Name

Date of Test

Please mark like this ⊢.

PUPIL NUMBER					
[0]	[0]	[0]	[0]	[0]	[0]
[1]	[1]	[1]	[1]	[1]	[1]
[2]	[2]	[2]	[2]	[2]	[2]
[3]	[3]	[3]	[3]	[3]	[3]
[4]	[4]	[4]	[4]	[4]	[4]
[5]	[5]	[5]	[5]	[5]	[5]
[6]	[6]	[6]	[6]	[6]	[6]
[7]	[7]	[7]	[7]	[7]	[7]
[8]	[8]	[8]	[8]	[8]	[8]
[9]	[9]	[9]	[9]	[9]	[9]

SCHOOL NUMBER					
[0]	[0]	[0]	[0]	[0]	[0]
[1]	[1]	[1]	[1]	[1]	[1]
[2]	[2]	[2]	[2]	[2]	[2]
[3]	[3]	[3]	[3]	[3]	[3]
[4]	[4]	[4]	[4]	[4]	[4]
[5]	[5]	[5]	[5]	[5]	[5]
[6]	[6]	[6]	[6]	[6]	[6]
[7]	[7]	[7]	[7]	[7]	[7]
[8]	[8]	[8]	[8]	[8]	[8]
[9]	[9]	[9]	[9]	[9]	[9]

DATE OF BIRTH				
Day		Month		Year
[0]	[0]	January ▭		1990 ▭
[1]	[1]	February ▭		1991 ▭
[2]	[2]	March ▭		1992 ▭
[3]	[3]	April ▭		1993 ▭
	[4]	May ▭		1994 ▭
	[5]	June ▭		1995 ▭
	[6]	July ▭		1996 ▭
	[7]	August ▭		1997 ▭
	[8]	September ▭		1998 ▭
	[9]	October ▭		1999 ▭
		November ▭		2000 ▭
		December ▭		2001 ▭

The Story of Jean Lafitte

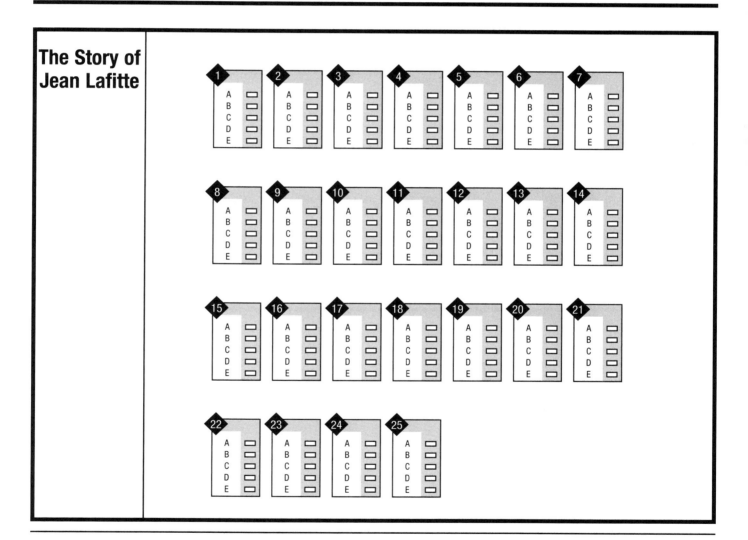

The Journey

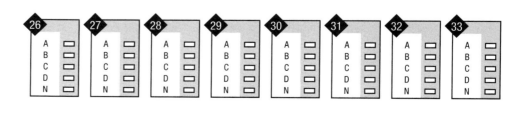

PUPIL NUMBER

[0]	[0]	[0]	[0]	[0]	[0]
[1]	[1]	[1]	[1]	[1]	[1]
[2]	[2]	[2]	[2]	[2]	[2]
[3]	[3]	[3]	[3]	[3]	[3]
[4]	[4]	[4]	[4]	[4]	[4]
[5]	[5]	[5]	[5]	[5]	[5]
[6]	[6]	[6]	[6]	[6]	[6]
[7]	[7]	[7]	[7]	[7]	[7]
[8]	[8]	[8]	[8]	[8]	[8]
[9]	[9]	[9]	[9]	[9]	[9]

Fred's Holiday

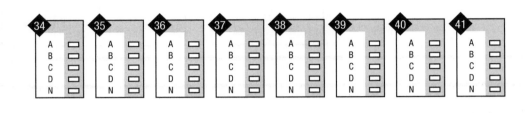

Painting for Money

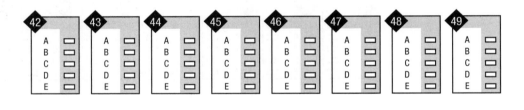

Pupil's Name		Date of Test

School Name

Please mark like this ⊢.

PUPIL NUMBER	SCHOOL NUMBER
[0] [0] [0] [0] [0] [0]	[0] [0] [0] [0] [0] [0]
[1] [1] [1] [1] [1] [1]	[1] [1] [1] [1] [1] [1]
[2] [2] [2] [2] [2] [2]	[2] [2] [2] [2] [2] [2]
[3] [3] [3] [3] [3] [3]	[3] [3] [3] [3] [3] [3]
[4] [4] [4] [4] [4] [4]	[4] [4] [4] [4] [4] [4]
[5] [5] [5] [5] [5] [5]	[5] [5] [5] [5] [5] [5]
[6] [6] [6] [6] [6] [6]	[6] [6] [6] [6] [6] [6]
[7] [7] [7] [7] [7] [7]	[7] [7] [7] [7] [7] [7]
[8] [8] [8] [8] [8] [8]	[8] [8] [8] [8] [8] [8]
[9] [9] [9] [9] [9] [9]	[9] [9] [9] [9] [9] [9]

DATE OF BIRTH

Day		Month	Year
[0]	[0]	January	1990
[1]	[1]	February	1991
[2]	[2]	March	1992
[3]	[3]	April	1993
	[4]	May	1994
	[5]	June	1995
	[6]	July	1996
	[7]	August	1997
	[8]	September	1998
	[9]	October	1999
		November	2000
		December	2001

Michelle's Holiday

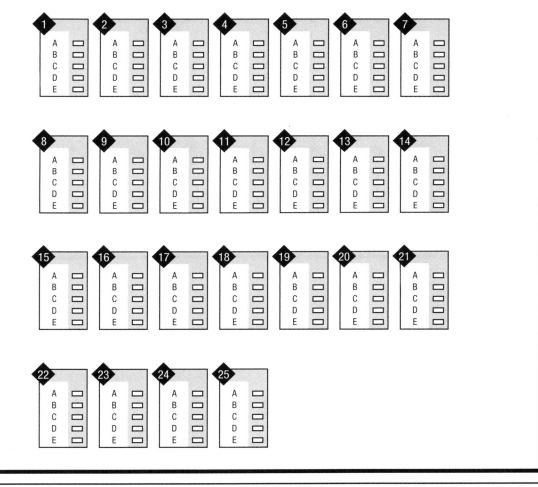

The Knight's Journey

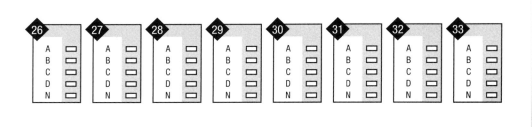

Lucie's Bike Ride

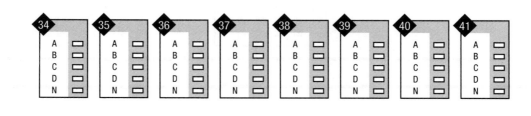

The Concert

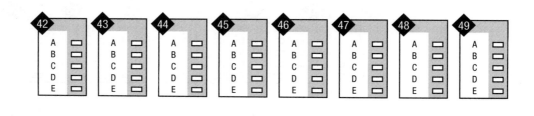

Pupil's Name

School Name

Date of Test

DATE OF BIRTH

Day		Month		Year	
[0]	[0]	January ☐		1990 ☐	
[1]	[1]	February ☐		1991 ☐	
[2]	[2]	March ☐		1992 ☐	
[3]	[3]	April ☐		1993 ☐	
	[4]	May ☐		1994 ☐	
	[5]	June ☐		1995 ☐	
	[6]	July ☐		1996 ☐	
	[7]	August ☐		1997 ☐	
	[8]	September ☐		1998 ☐	
	[9]	October ☐		1999 ☐	
		November ☐		2000 ☐	
		December ☐		2001 ☐	

PUPIL NUMBER

[0] [0] [0] [0] [0] [0]
[1] [1] [1] [1] [1] [1]
[2] [2] [2] [2] [2] [2]
[3] [3] [3] [3] [3] [3]
[4] [4] [4] [4] [4] [4]
[5] [5] [5] [5] [5] [5]
[6] [6] [6] [6] [6] [6]
[7] [7] [7] [7] [7] [7]
[8] [8] [8] [8] [8] [8]
[9] [9] [9] [9] [9] [9]

SCHOOL NUMBER

[0] [0] [0] [0] [0] [0] [0]
[1] [1] [1] [1] [1] [1] [1]
[2] [2] [2] [2] [2] [2] [2]
[3] [3] [3] [3] [3] [3] [3]
[4] [4] [4] [4] [4] [4] [4]
[5] [5] [5] [5] [5] [5] [5]
[6] [6] [6] [6] [6] [6] [6]
[7] [7] [7] [7] [7] [7] [7]
[8] [8] [8] [8] [8] [8] [8]
[9] [9] [9] [9] [9] [9] [9]

Please mark like this ⊢.

The Story of Robin Hood

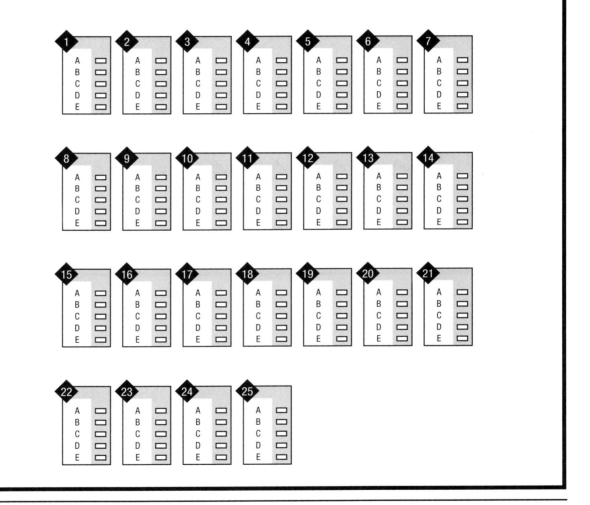

The Big Match

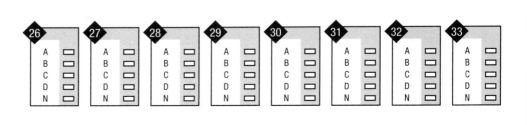

PUPIL NUMBER

[0]	[0]	[0]	[0]	[0]	[0]
[1]	[1]	[1]	[1]	[1]	[1]
[2]	[2]	[2]	[2]	[2]	[2]
[3]	[3]	[3]	[3]	[3]	[3]
[4]	[4]	[4]	[4]	[4]	[4]
[5]	[5]	[5]	[5]	[5]	[5]
[6]	[6]	[6]	[6]	[6]	[6]
[7]	[7]	[7]	[7]	[7]	[7]
[8]	[8]	[8]	[8]	[8]	[8]
[9]	[9]	[9]	[9]	[9]	[9]

Hide and Seek

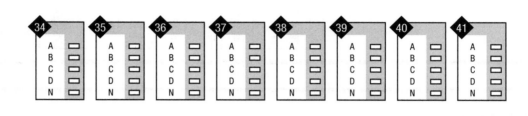

The Secret

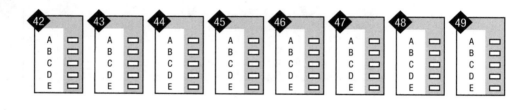

Pupil's Name

School Name

Date of Test

© Letts Educational Ltd

Please mark like this ⊢.

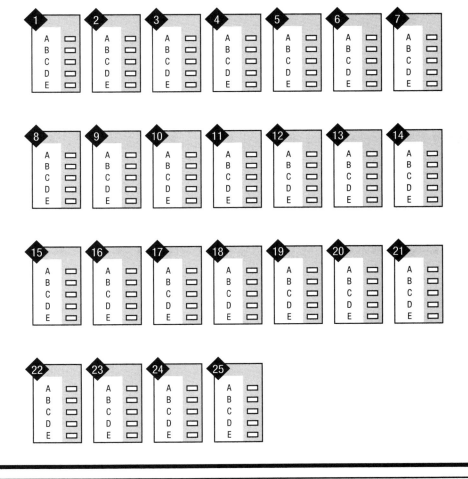

The Story of Ancient Rome

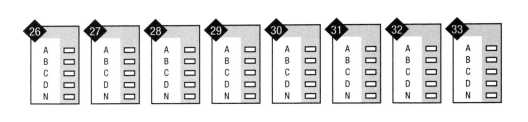

The Sea Journey

The First Day

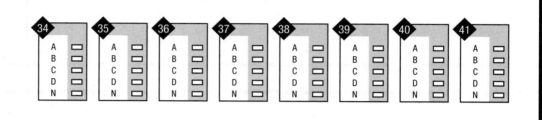

The Spooky House

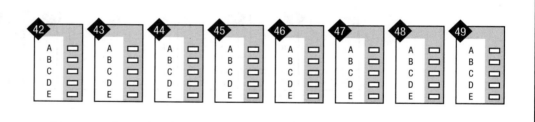